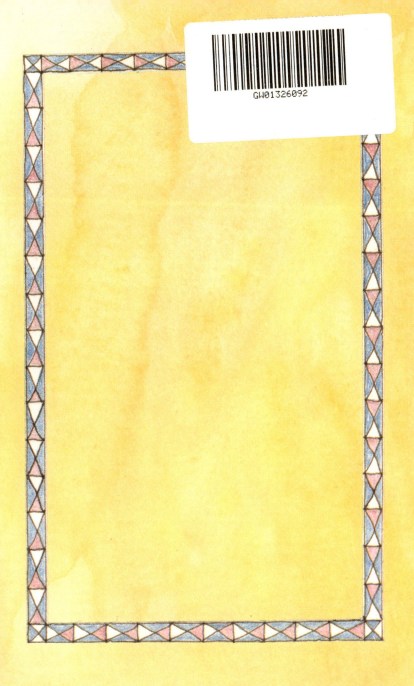

NOTE TO PARENTS

This familiar Bible story has been retold in a sensitive and simple way so that young children can read and understand it for themselves. But the special message of the story remains unchanged. It is the message of God's love and care for us all.

The First Christmas

retold by Marjorie Newman
illustrated by Edgar Hodges

Copyright © MCMLXXXVIII by World International Publishing Limited.
All rights reserved.
Published in Great Britain by World International Publishing Limited.
An Egmont Company, Egmont House,
P.O. Box 111, Great Ducie Street,
Manchester M60 3BL.
Printed in DDR.
ISBN 7235 3005 X

Once there was a donkey who lived in Nazareth. The donkey belonged to a man called Joseph. Joseph was kind, and the donkey loved him. But he loved Mary even more. Mary was going to be Joseph's wife.

One day, the donkey saw a bright light shining inside Mary's house. He could hear an angel speaking to Mary. "You are going to have a very special baby," the angel was saying. "He is God's own son. You must call Him Jesus."

The donkey was very excited. He wished he could tell Joseph, but Mary told him. At first, Joseph was puzzled, so God sent an angel to Joseph, too. Then Joseph understood. He and Mary began to get ready for the baby.

Some time later, the donkey heard Joseph say to Mary, "Everyone must go to the place where they were born, to be counted. We must go to Bethlehem. We'll go on the donkey."

Bethlehem! That was nearly a hundred miles! The donkey hoped he could do it ...

At last they were all ready to set out. Mary rode on his back. She carried a warm bundle of baby clothes, in case the special baby should be born while they were away from home.

At first, the donkey trotted along cheerfully. Clip, clop, clip, clop! But after a while, he grew very tired. Clip ... clop ... clip ... clop went his hooves. Mary was very tired, too. Joseph was worried. So many people were going to Bethlehem. Would they find anywhere to stay?

When they got to Bethlehem, the donkey was so tired, he could hardly put one foot in front of the other. He stopped outside an inn. Joseph knocked on the door.

"No room! No room!" called the innkeeper.

"But my wife is very tired!" said Joseph.

The innkeeper looked at Mary, and he was sorry for her. "You can sleep in the stable with the animals, if you like," he said.

"Thank you," said Joseph.

The donkey was happy. He liked being with Mary and Joseph.

There, in the stable, baby Jesus was born. Mary wrapped Him in the baby clothes. Joseph looked for a cosy place to put the baby. The donkey had been eating some hay from the manger. "Hee haw!" he said.

"You're right, donkey!" said Joseph. And he laid the baby in the manger on the soft, sweet-smelling hay. It was the very first Christmas night. And other people were awake, as well...

Out on the hills near Bethlehem shepherds were watching over their sheep.
Everything was very peaceful in the starlight.
Suddenly, there was a bright light in the sky!

The shepherds hid their faces in fear. Then they heard the beautiful voice of an angel, saying, "Don't be afraid! I have good news for you! A very special baby has been born in Bethlehem! He is God's own son! You will find Him lying in a manger." Then the sky was full of angels singing.

The angels' voices faded away. The only light came from the stars and the fire. The shepherds jumped up. "Did you see? Did you hear?" they cried. "Let us go and find this baby!" One stayed on guard, and the rest hurried along the road to Bethlehem.

The donkey was half asleep. Suddenly he woke up. Shepherds were in the stable, worshipping the baby as if He were a King.

"How did you know He was here?" Joseph asked them.

"The angels told us," they replied. The donkey nodded. He knew about angels.

The shepherds went back to their sheep. Next day, the innkeeper let Mary, Joseph and the baby Jesus stay in his house. The donkey was sad. But soon he was needed again. "We have to take the baby to the Temple Church in Jerusalem, so that God can bless Him there," Joseph explained.

The donkey waited outside the Temple Church. He saw some wise men ride by on camels. They were talking in excited voices. "We are looking for the new baby King," the wise men told the people. "We have followed His star from our own lands."

"The baby King is sure to be in the palace," said one wise man.

"No!" the donkey wanted to say. "We have the special baby here!" The wise men rode past. The donkey was upset; but he couldn't stop them. When the wise men reached the palace, they spoke to Herod, the King.

"What?" cried Herod. "A baby *King*?"

Herod's own wise men said, "The baby will be born in Bethlehem."

"Oh," said Herod. He looked at the visitors. "When you have found Him, tell me. I want to worship Him, too!" Really, Herod meant to have the baby killed. He didn't want a new King!

That night, the donkey couldn't sleep. Partly, he was worrying about the wise men. Partly, he was kept awake by the bright light of the star which shone over the stable.

Suddenly, he heard voices. Then he saw camels being brought into the yard. The wise men had found the baby! They were going into the innkeeper's house.

The wise men worshipped baby Jesus. They gave Him gifts – gold, frankincense and myrrh. And they didn't go back to King Herod. God sent them a dream, to warn them. They went home another way.

God sent a dream to Joseph, too. "You must take Mary and the baby, and escape to Egypt," said God. "Herod means to harm the child."

The donkey carried Mary and Jesus all the way to Egypt. They lived there until Jesus was about two years old. Then God sent Joseph another dream to tell him that King Herod was dead. It was safe to go home!

The donkey carried Mary and Jesus back to Nazareth. The donkey still loved Joseph. He still loved Mary. But he loved the boy Jesus best of all.

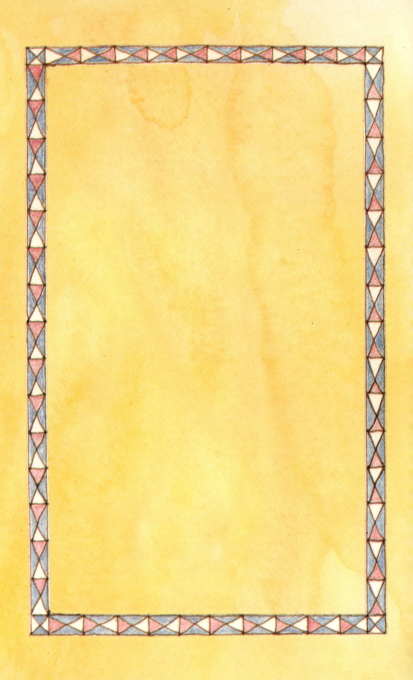